To Serve the Present Age

To Serve the Present Age

A Practical Guide to Church Growth and Development

CARLTON R. WORTHEN

Carlton Worthen Publishing, Atlanta, GA

ISBN- 9781092349772

Library of Congress Control Number: 2019904493

Printed In USA

Atlanta, GA

Dedicated to my father

The Reverend Charlie Worthen, M.Div.

TABLE OF CONTENTS

INTRODUCTION

In this day and age, how do we promote growth within the church? How do we extend the church beyond its four walls and draw in people who are lost and hurting? How do we reach people who might never have come inside a church building? How do we reach people who might have never heard of the name "Jesus Christ?"

To those of us who were raised up within the Christian faith, the idea that others might be ignorant of Jesus' plan for their salvation can be unfathomable. This is especially true in this era ruled by technology that seems to connect people from throughout the world in the blink of an eye.

There are many people who are spiritually lost and in pain. Therefore, as church leaders we must always ask ourselves, how can I be used by God as his agent to offer Christ to people who are hurting and lost?

We must never become complacent with the number of people we see within the four walls of the church each Sunday. Rather, Jesus challenges us to rise up and have a passion to want to serve those within the community who are spiritually lost. The question, of course, is how? I believe the answer lies in spreading the message of Christ's grace throughout the world. We must reach out to others with empathy. At the same time, we must employ technology and the application of practical aid and advice to those who are in desperate need, both for the necessities of life and for Jesus' salvation.

This is the philosophy I will bring to the office of Executive Director for Church Growth and Development within the African Methodist Episcopal Church.

Throughout this book I will outline for you five essential principles that I have employed at St. John AME in Eufaula, AL that has helped to spark phenomenal church growth. I firmly believe that if you employ these principals throughout your ministry, you also will begin to notice a significant growth.

The five principles are dynamic and engaging thematic worship, giving as a form of worship, technology to serve the present age, strategic community partnerships, and holistic ministry.

Planting seeds for global growth

What does the office of Executive Director for Church Growth and Development entail? In this office, it will be my responsibility to work with congregations throughout the denomination to search for ways local congregations can grow.

However, it is important to remember that the AME Church stretches across multiple continents, encompassing the globe. I want to plant more churches throughout the world. Our denomination has a global outreach and follows the instruction of Jesus Christ laid out in the New Testament.

> *"And then he told them, 'Go into all the world and preach the Good News to everyone. Anyone who believes and is baptized will be saved. But anyone who refuses to believe will be damned. These miraculous signs will accompany those who believe: They will cast out demons in my name, and they will speak in new languages. They will be able to handle snakes with safety, and if they drink anything poisonous, it won't hurt them. They will be able to place their hands on the sick, and they will be healed.'*
>
> *"When the Lord Jesus had finished talking with them, he was taken up into heaven and sat down in the place of honor at God's right hand. And the disciples went everywhere and preached, and the Lord worked through them, confirming what they said by many miraculous signs."*
> Mark 16:15-20 (NLT)

Currently the African Methodist Episcopal Church reaches into the Caribbean, Europe, Africa and India to plant churches. These are all places with vastly different cultures, perspectives and world-views. How can one denomination approach such contrasting landscapes with the singular goal of winning people over to Christ, establishing and growing congregations?

What we must always remember is the globe is comprised of many cultures, not to mention many different people with vastly contrasting values, beliefs and personalities. However, there is but one Savior, Jesus Christ, who died and who was risen three days later. Jesus who is the gift of salvation is the unifying aspect offered for every single person on Earth. Regardless of nation, culture or language, Jesus is the answer for everyone.

People throughout the world are still crying out for spiritual salvation just as they were when Jesus came to Earth. This position, this office for Church Growth and Development, is for such a time as this. Our world still needs to know that as dark and dim as things may seem, Christ is the light that will lead us all out of darkness.

However, we must acknowledge and tailor outreach strategies that address different people from different environments and cultures. We must understand that everyone has not been afforded the same opportunities in life as others have. We must be cognitively aware that a person's environment and how they were raised greatly influences their outlook when it comes to faith.

We cannot dismiss the impact one's culture has on them. A person's culture greatly effects and impacts their worldview. A person's upbringing, environment and exposure to others cultures and perspectives have a great impact on one's personality, perspective, beliefs and values.

Hindu is the predominant religion in India; Islam is the predominant religion in many areas of the world. The AME Church seeks to build congregations all over the globe. We must consider the cultural impact different religions have on particular regions of the world.

But this challenge can also be counted as a blessing and an opportunity for us seeking to spread the Gospel. We must educate ourselves on the cultures and environments we set out into to spread Jesus' message of salvation. The more understanding we are of other people's experiences and environments, the more inclined we are to be understanding of why Jesus' gift of grace is so important and why it unifies everyone on the planet no matter their country or culture.

America is a mission field as well

I really want America to understand we should not feel that we have a position of superiority when it comes to church growth and development. Churches in other nations are growing at a faster rate. Pew Research Center studies reveal that the United States should be considered a mission field, in fact. This is why we must not abandon America as a prospective mission field or an opportunity to spread the Gospel.

What is the reason for the decline in church attendance in the United States? Some of the many causes for decline

xiv CARLTON R. WORTHEN

are race and socio-economic status. When you put those in the pot, and the feelings of isolation and alienation they breed in people, that becomes a recipe ripe for decline.

Meet people where they are

The AME Church spans all throughout the world. However, the way of reaching out to people to win them over to Christ, grow churches and develop congregations should remain generally the same. Evangelism and outreach must be done on a very personal level, reaching people on a one-on-one basis.

As Executive Director of Church Growth and Development I will bring a very unique and empathetic perspective when it comes to evangelism and outreach. My philosophy on evangelism is this: you have to be willing to meet people where they are. Whether you are in Gaborone, Botswana or Birmingham, Alabama, you must empathize with a person on a personal level in order to make them understand the gift of Jesus' grace through you. And you must do this in a compassionate, tactful and nonjudgmental manner.

A disciple of Christ, seeking to spread Jesus' message of salvation, must be spiritually discerning. Spiritual discernment means you have to make certain when you go in and begin to evangelize to someone that you must not come across as condemning people.

For example, if I am out canvassing neighborhoods and I see some people drinking from beer cans and using coarse language, that is not the time to be condemning their lifestyle choices. No, this is an opportunity to pray with and for people.

I will ask these people: "Is there anything I can pray with you for?" "Do you have a family member who needs prayer?" And then I will shake their hand while they hold their beer in the other hand.

Another example is if I came across a young girl who is pregnant. She has tattoos all over her body, on her arms and neck. I will not say to her: "Who made you pregnant?" or "Don't you know that having sex before marriage is a sin?" I will ask her if I can help her or pray for her.

When I see a new person in my church who wears clothes that are always worn and tattered, speaks very loudly or uses coarse language, I wouldn't dare say that person doesn't have a good relationship with God. Because I do not understand their background or experiences. I must not pass judgment on them based on their appearance.

When you are trying to spread the message of Christ's salvation to a hurting world and bring people into the church, do not criticize them or be judgmental.

Be empathetic, compassionate, kind and spiritually discerning when trying to reach out to the lost. Remember that Jesus would talk to, help and save whoever he came across, regardless of their class and/or position in society. Christ consorted with the lowest of the low in the society he lived in during his time on Earth.

> *"Tax collectors and other notorious sinners often came to listen to Jesus teach. This made the Pharisees and teachers of religious law complain that he was associating with such sinful people - even eating with them!*
>
> *"So Jesus told them this story: 'If a man has a hundred sheep and one of them gets lost, what will he do? Won't he leave the ninety-nine others in the wilderness and go to search for the one that is lost until he finds it? And when he has found it, he will joyfully carry it home on his shoulders. When he arrives, he will call together his friends and neighbors, saying, "Rejoice with me because I have found my lost sheep." In the same way, there is more joy in heaven over one lost sinner who repents and returns to God than over ninety-nine others who are righteous and haven't strayed away!'"* Luke 15:1-7 (NLT)

Empathy is the key. This is the attitude we must take while spreading the Gospel and building our churches: "But for the grace of God, there go I. I very well could be in those same situations." I could very well have a disease, mental illness, be homeless or hungry but for the grace of God.

What inspires me daily is to know that someone who is going through a difficult season in their life knows that Jesus loves them. I am constantly preaching a theology of hope.

This accepting, nonjudgmental attitude forges a rapport of trust with those you seek to reach with the message of Jesus' salvation.

Grace, empathy, holistic ministries, technology are keys

Whatever it is they're going through, communicate how Christ speaks to you in that moment to help lost people. That help may come in the form of prayer and other means of spiritual guidance. However, that aid to the lost may also come through a practical gesture. Feeding a hungry person a meal, giving them clothing, companionship, providing them an opportunity for a dynamic worship experience or educating them on a certain topic to help them survive are as important as prayer. These ministries will provide the basic necessities of life to those who need them.

In these following chapters, I will expound upon what I believe are five key points for church growth: dynamic engaging thematic worship, giving as a form of worship, strategic community partnerships, holistic ministries, and utilizing technology to grow a congregation and promote outreach. These, along with a spirit of discernment and empathy when reaching the lost, are the factors I want to bring to the office of Executive Director of Church Growth and Development.

Holistic ministries expand the church beyond its four walls, drawing people into the church by aiding them with practical help and advice. Strategic community partnerships and employing technology help fuel this outreach. Dynamic thematic worship, and financial giving offers newcomers and congregants a worship experience like no other.

I am seeking the office of Executive Director of Church Growth and Development because I believe the practical tools I am offering congregations will help them experience explosive dynamic growth. Why should we watch churches or see individuals struggle to grow when we can provide them with practical tools to grow? That is what I am offering. I am offering to whosoever desires - just try it for 90 days, all of the plans and suggestions I have laid out in this book, and see what happens.

Use the unifying message of grace. Employ empathy when reaching others. Use holistic ministries and technology as tools to expand outreach and grow our churches. With these outreach techniques, I believe the AME Church will see its congregations grow beyond their wildest imagination.

1

DYNAMIC AND ENGAGING THEMATIC WORSHIP

"O God, you are my God; I earnestly search for you. My soul thirsts for you; my whole-body longs for you in this parched and weary land where there is no water.

"I have seen you in your sanctuary and gazed upon your power and glory. Your unfailing love is better than life itself; how I praise you! I will praise you as long as I live, lifting up my hands to you in prayer. You satisfy me more than the richest feast. I will praise you with songs of joy.

"I lie awake thinking of you, meditating on you through the night. Because you are my helper, I sing for joy in the shadow of your wings. I cling to you; your strong right hand holds me securely.

"But those plotting to destroy me will come to ruin. They will go down into the depths of the earth. They will die by the sword and become the food of jackals. But the king will rejoice with God. All who swear to tell the truth will praise him, while liars will be silenced." Psalm 63:1-11 (NLT)

Consider the following people: An eighty-year-old woman with a fourth-grade education. A professor with a PhD. A spouse struggling to keep her marriage together. A convicted felon who has served his time. The recovering drug addict. The cancer patient undergoing chemotherapy. These are all people who could and do walk inside a church searching for answers, seeking to worship the Lord in the midst of their struggles.

These are all people with very different backgrounds, perspectives and challenges. How does a worship experience go about reaching each and every one of them?

I believe the solution lies in thematic worship.

What is thematic worship?
My own personal definition of "thematic worship" refers to an entire worship experience that is centered around one theological theme. Please do not confuse the term "thematic worship" with "worship" itself. Worship is defined by someone seeking to have an encounter with God. Worship is also seeking answers from God in the midst of your struggles. The key word in that definition

is "struggles," plural - different challenges face different people.

Thematic worship does all it can to reach out to everyone in the congregation. A thematic worship experience makes every effort to make every song, litany, skit and call to worship center around a specific theme. Therefore, the experience reaches out to as many people in as many ways as possible to help them understand its theme and grow closer to God.

Thematic worship also gives a streamlined focused approach to the worship experience. No one in the church - those listening or those who created and composed the worship experience - loses sight of its theme or goal. The message is instilled in the congregation.

Examples of thematic worship done at St. John AME recently include worship experiences with themes such as "Praise," "Reset" and "New Things." Hence every single aspect of the worship experience centers on these specific themes. That doesn't just mean a sermon or a song preached or sung on Sunday respectively. That also includes Bible studies done throughout the week, banners hung in the sanctuary and online hashtag campaigns. All of this can assist in making the theme much more focused and dynamic for the worship experience.

Why is thematic worship effective?

Thematic worship helps benefit the individual. First of all, it doesn't leave them with a scattered, unfocused or rushed-sounding worship experience. Oftentimes people enter into the sanctuary feeling troubled and lost in their struggles as it is. They need a clear objective - the worship experience's theme to rally around. The thematic worship experience does not deviate away from its theme. It gives the congregation an unswerving goal to focus on in connecting with God.

Second, with thematic worship, you can incorporate many different ways of reaching the congregation with a specific theme. You are not limited to a sermon or a few hymns. Litanies, praise dancers and skits can also be incorporated into the worship experience.

It may be litanies; it may be the praise dancers. It may be the sermon that reaches an individual in the congregation. Every person who is seeing or hearing the worship experience is being touched by one theme.

Thematic worship demands planning

Thematic worship cannot be done on the fly. The worship experience can and does allow for the Holy Spirit to move through the congregation in surprising ways, as I'll discuss later on in this chapter. However, on the whole, thematic worship is dependent on intensive and collaborative planning.

That planning begins with the head of the church - the pastor.

Over the years, I have learned about designing the worship experience. And let me tell you, the thematic worship experience literally starts with a whole lot of prayer.

I tell young preachers this: Don't stand above people in your congregation, stand in the middle of them. I think what happens with many teachers of Christianity is they have good theology. However, they cannot connect with people from all walks of life - from Miss Edith, an elderly lady with a grammar school education to Dr. Winston, a university professor.

Step into their shoes. See the world from their perspective. Then begin to pray and meditate on how to best connect with them through a worship experience, of which your sermon will play a major role.

Prayerfully plan the sermon

As a pastor, my "radar," so to speak, is always up, searching for people in need of spiritual care and the challenges they face. Stand in the middle of the struggles people are going through. Ask yourself what you are giving to people to encourage them in the times we're living in. This is always the mindset I take when writing my sermons.

The sermon with great care and prayer should be planned and thoroughly exegeted.

In creating sermons, I exhaustively study the scriptures connected to the theme. Every single word must be exegeted in the original language and made relevant to today. I use a special Logos Bible software package for exegetical purposes. Imagine sixteen tractor trailer trucks pulling up to your house, each loaded with books, commentaries and dictionaries - this is a fitting analogy for my exegetical software. It's a massive and powerful library I use for all my sermon and Bible study work.

Researching a topic thoroughly is important. If you have not planned the sermon studiously, the congregation will know. However, to truly connect with the congregation through a sermon and worship experience, be keenly aware of the congregants' individual struggles and the social, political and social climate they live in.

Make thematic worship relevant to the present age

Be real. That's how you start reaching people. Put stories from the Bible in a current social, political and cultural context. The story of Mary, the mother of Jesus, is a very familiar one in our culture. Perhaps even to someone who has never been to church. But when you step back and really examine the familiar story, you can see it from a new perspective.

Just think about it - Mary, a virgin, is visited by a supernatural being, an angel. That in and of itself is mind-blowing. Then the angel informs her that she will give birth to the Messiah!

Now, relate the story of Mary in a way anyone in this day and age will understand. Mary was considered to be someone from the lower class. In today's society, Mary would have lived in the trailer park, the housing project, the ghetto. She didn't grow up in a mansion.

Draw that bridge. Put Mary's story, Moses' story or David's story in a context to make it relevant to people in the present day. Then they can see those stories of old from their perspective.

The worship experience is an opportunity to connect scriptures with current political, cultural and social issues. Make the worship experience a learning experience as well. This also is an opportunity to expose the congregation to new and relevant information and resources.

During the month of February, Black History Month, St. John AME Church puts a very heavy emphasis on black people in the Bible. The Black National Anthem is also played. Eufaula, Alabama, where I currently pastor, is a small rural community surrounded by cotton fields. The Black National Anthem is not played before every basketball or football game here.

The song's lyrics include:

> *"We have come, treading our path through the blood*
> *of the slaughtered,*
> *Out from the gloomy past,*
> *Till now we stand at last*
> *Where the white gleam of our bright star is cast."*

As a pastor, I would be at fault if I didn't expose my children to this important piece of their heritage and struggle as black people. (I consider all the youth of St. John AME as my children whom I love dearly.)

During October, Domestic Violence Awareness Month, the drama ministry performs skits about domestic violence every Sunday. These skits are coordinated with the sermon and the rest of the worship experience to focus on this important and relevant topic.

Thematic worship demands collaboration

Once I have pondered the sermon theme, I get with my worship leader, music ministry team and drama ministry. We brainstorm different songs, hymns, dances and skits to use in the worship experience to coordinate with the sermon. It's important to know that the planned worship experience is tentative at this point. This is largely due to the fact that you may not have all of the pieces figured out to ensure that the worship experience is memorable. However, the pastor is encouraged to at a minimum know the theme as well as the scripture that will be used in order for the collaboration process to be beneficial.

In thematic worship, we must make every effort to make every song, litany, skit and call to worship center around a specific theme. That means everyone who is a part of the collaboration process must be on the same page.

Various graphics to be displayed on screens must be researched and designed. The drama ministry has to rehearse skits. The dance ministry has to have music to connect with the theme. Everyone must have an understanding of the text to be referenced. The choir must get psalms and hymns together; the choir may have to learn contemporary songs they aren't aware of. Planning is extensive and intensive. The pastor's knowledge of the source material must be passed on to those they collaborate with so the congregation is aware of their dedication to the service.

Collaboration is key to creating a thematic worship experience. It requires trust among the pastor, minister of music and any other church leaders involved in the planning process. This is because, though planning and coordination is important, we must make room for the Holy Spirit to move throughout the worship experience - sometimes in surprising ways.

During a recent worship experience, our minister of music, who is also a gospel recording artist, wrote and performed a song right at the conclusion of an invitation to discipleship/altar call and our musicians got right behind it. The song was connected to the theme of the worship experience; it naturally flowed with the course of the service and was not out of order.

The above gives credence to two points: First, my implicit trust of the church leaders who assist me with the planning of the worship experience alongside their trust in me. It is absolutely imperative that the worship leaders and pastor have a close working relationship.

Second, this displays the fact that the Holy Spirit is moving through our planning process, so we are prepared if - and when - the Holy Spirit does move throughout the worship experience in impromptu ways.

Songs play an influential role

In the Bible, there is a passage regarding Satan himself being leader of the Lord's music ministry. He got beside himself and was thrown out of heaven when he began to think more highly of himself along with a lot of the choir!

"You were the model of perfection,
full of wisdom and exquisite in beauty.
You were in Eden,
the garden of God.
Your clothing was adorned with every precious stone -
red carnelian, pale-green peridot, white moonstone,
blue-green beryl, onyx, green jasper,
blue lapis lazuli, turquoise, and emerald -
all beautifully crafted for you
and set in the finest gold.
They were given to you
on the day you were created.
I ordained and anointed you
as the mighty angelic guardian.
You had access to the holy mountain of God
and walked among the stones of fire.
You were blameless in all you did
from the day you were created
until the day evil was found in you.
Your rich commerce led you to violence,
and you sinned.

*So I banished you in disgrace
from the mountain of God.
I expelled you, O mighty guardian,
from your place among the stones of fire.
Your heart was filled with pride
because of all your beauty.
Your wisdom was corrupted
by your love of splendor.
So I threw you to the ground
and exposed you to the curious gaze of kings.
You defiled your sanctuaries
with your sins and your dishonest trade.
So I brought fire out from within you,
and it consumed you.
I reduced you to ashes on the ground
in the sight of all who were watching.
All who knew you are appalled at your fate.
You have come to a terrible end,
and you will exist no more."* Ezekiel 28:12-19
(NLT)

The above points out what an influential role the music ministry plays in the worship experience. Who doesn't love a catchy song and beat? Music can make a worshiper feel motivated, inspired and reflective. However, make sure the focus remains on God and not the music itself. Music has the potential to dominate the worship experience. In fact, some of the biggest struggles and disagreements in a church often come out of the music ministry. Remember, however, that no one element - be it the sermon, music or drama - should dominate the worship experience.

People who come to worship do not come to be entertained. It is not the role of the choir to perform like Beyoncé or Garth Brooks. The choir is there to give reverence to God, not for people's praise or approval.

Music is a powerful tool for reaching out to people. But like all tools, it can be used to enhance the worship experience or to distract the congregation from connecting with God. Make sure it achieves the former.

You might have been to a Christmas cantata and heard the choir sing "Jingle Bells" or "Rudolph the Red-Nosed Reindeer." These songs are festive songs prevalent in our culture, but they have no kind of reference to Christ, God or the Holy Spirit; they have no place in a worship experience.

All songs incorporated in a worship experience must be theologically sound. If not, the congregation will lose focus on God. Personally, cannot go wrong with a hymn. It usually connects directly with scripture.

Nevertheless, more contemporary songs may be used in the worship experience as well. Many people in the AME tradition believe the first song in the worship experience to be lifted up has to be a hymn of praise. However, so long as the first song lifted up is a song of adoration and praise to God, it is appropriate. At St. John AME, we sing a wide variety of contemporary songs as the first song of the worship experience. These include: "Every Praise is to Our God," "O Give Thanks," "Our God is Awesome," "Way Maker" and "O Magnify the Lord for He's Worthy to be Praised" just to name a few. So long as these are songs solely of adoration and praise to God and not just focused on we as people getting our blessings, they are suitable.

I tell my flock don't fold your arms and begin to pout and say we're not doing it the "AME way." This leads me to my next point that can involve music in the worship experience.

Don't turn traditions into idols

An idol isn't necessarily an antiquated statue or graven image. An idol is anything we exalt above God to the point that it prohibits us from connecting with God. Traditions in the church can easily fall down that slippery slope because the congregation exalts them above God.

At St. John, during the 11:00 a.m. worship experience, the Decalogue is recited only on fourth Sundays. It is no longer done during every Sunday morning worship. However, we now have the youth to lead the Summary of the Decalogue on fourth Sundays which is Youth Sunday. We do the Decalogue every Sunday during Sunday school. I had several confrontations with people about this. They became bent out of shape that I was changing this tradition.

I tell them to get out of bed early enough to come to Sunday school!

They were placing the focus on the tradition itself, not on glorifying God through it. Don't be bound by idolatry, but don't disrespect or disregard traditions. Traditions definitely have their place in worship; that place is to always remind us where we come from and why we do what we do. Traditions can also anchor you in clarity. They should not be pushed aside, but do not make them the focus.

Like music, traditions should be a tool to worship God.

Be open to new approaches of worship
Jesus states in the Bible:

> *"Healthy people don't need a doctor - sick people do. I have come to call not those who think they are righteous, but those who know they are sinners."* Mark 2:17 (NLT)

When a congregation is comprised predominantly of people who have been brought up in a church setting they already know the order of worship. They already know all the lyrics to the songs sung during worship. They are familiar with scriptures and litanies.

In order to grow, however, a church must begin attracting others beyond its congregation. Some of these newcomers might not have set foot inside a church before. They are unfamiliar with songs, litanies and scriptures which established congregants know well.

This is why it's imperative that an unchurched person needs to be engaged in the most efficient, effective way possible.

Do not take it for granted that everyone entering your sanctuary or viewing a worship experience in any capacity (online or otherwise) is familiar with the Bible. I am always mindful of the person who is unchurched. They may not be familiar with the Bible, lyrics to (what we might consider) "familiar" songs, litanies or scriptures.

During a worship experience at St. John AME, everything - every Bible verse, every song lyric - is projected on overhead screens to be viewed by all. This is to get a point clearly across.

A pastor may speak faster than a person can take notes. If they cannot write it down that fast, I encourage worshipers and visitors to use their smartphones to take a picture of the overhead screen with a verse or passage displayed.

It is not uncommon at all for me to tell congregants to take a picture during a worship experience, post it to Facebook and share it with their friends.

Make the worship experience as interactive as possible. Yes, encourage those in the audience to go back, read and research the Bible passages covered in their own private study time. During the worship experience, however, get your point across to them as clearly as possible.

St. John AME has invested a great deal in incorporating technology into the worship experience. In the past few years, the church has established an audio/visual room, wi-fi services throughout the campus, overhead screens in the sanctuary and a broad social media presence. Worship is now Livestreamed through the church website and social media platforms.

The church has focused a lot of resources to build this technology base into its worship experience. And it has reaped bountiful blessings. St. John has grown in leaps and bounds in the span of a few years. People have come through our doors, some from the surrounding community and others from as far away as Montgomery, Alabama and Tallahassee, Florida.

I remember a time when there were barely 30 people in the sanctuary on Sunday morning, but now hundreds of people have joined St. John AME. Countless people have been baptized and have given their lives to Christ. Many more have been encouraged in their faith. And these technological improvements have played a big part in this growth in reaching out to as many people as possible.

Be sensitive to how different people worship God
In the Bible, Moses asks to see God's face.

> *"The Lord replied, 'I will make all my goodness pass before you, and I will call out my name, Yahweh,*

before you. For I will show mercy to anyone I choose, and I will show compassion to anyone I choose. But you may not look directly at my face, for no one may see me and live.' The Lord continued, 'Look, stand near me on this rock. As my glorious presence passes by, I will hide you in the crevice of the rock and cover you with my hand until I have passed by. Then I will remove my hand and let you see me from behind. But my face will not be seen.'" Exodus 33:17-23 (NLT)

What a powerful message! It helps illustrate how God reaches people in different ways through different means of worship. Step into the shoes of your congregants; you will have a look at their faith on display by witnessing their own unique "style" of worship with God.

Recently, during a worship experience at St. John AME, I witnessed my baby sister worshiping God two days after chemotherapy. She still fought through her struggles to worship.

That is what worship means: You may have issues with God. You might even be angry at God in your struggles, but you still have not renounced your faith. Worship means finding God in the midst of your struggles. I see people every Sunday whose lives are just falling apart, but they still press their way on to worship.

Be sensitive to the fact, however, that all people worship God differently. If someone chooses to shout, they should not be frowned upon. If someone chooses to sit or stand quietly, they should not be judged. Worship is private as well as corporate. Some people may not always be receptive to touching their neighbor, giving them a hug or a high-five.

Worship is not always loud or demonstrative. Some people shed tears. Some meditate silently or simply lift a hand. These are all acts of worship. The quadriplegic whose hands and feet cannot move can worship. Even the prostitute and dope addict can worship God by acknowledging that without the presence of God in their life, they will not be able to move beyond their own shortcomings.

Through a dynamic worship experience, however, with many different elements reaching out to inspire and motivate the congregants, it will be hard to not participate when the Holy Spirit gets high. When the person sitting next to you is actively encouraging you, before you know it you'll be singing. Before you know it, you'll be crying. Before you know it, you'll be an active participant as well. Because a church functions not only as a canvas to explore your relationship with God. It is also an extended family that provides empathy and support.

You may come into a worship experience feeling down, depressed and frustrated. A connection with God as well as the encouragement from others will provide a balm to your soul.

A dynamic thematic worship experience will encourage a person's particular "style" of connecting with God. It will also encourage their participation in a group celebration with other congregants. Throughout this, they will remain focused on God and the theme throughout the worship experience. A thematic worship experience strives to - and does - touch each and every person in the congregation.

2

GIVING AS A FORM OF WORSHIP

In the Old Testament, Abraham (then known as Abram) encounters Melchizedek, the king of Salem, after a successful rescue of Abram's nephew Lot and his family. Melchizedek, who is described as a "priest of God Most High," blesses Abram. Melchizedek then blesses God.

> *"Melchizedek blessed Abram with this blessing:*
> *'Blessed be Abram by God Most High, Creator of heaven and earth. And blessed be God Most High, who has defeated your enemies for you.'*
> *"Then Abram gave Melchizedek a tenth of all the goods he had recovered. The king of Sodom said to Abram, 'Give back my people who were captured.*

> *But you may keep for yourself all the goods you have recovered.'*
>
> *"Abram replied to the king of Sodom, 'I solemnly swear to the Lord, God Most High, Creator of heaven and earth, that I will not take so much as a single thread or sandal thong from what belongs to you. Otherwise you might say, "I am the one who made Abram rich."'*" Genesis 14:19-23 (NLT)

This is the first time we hear about "tithing" in the Bible. The tithe is ten percent of everything you earn back to God. The tithe is also considered sacred and should never be compromised in any way. Abram gave a tenth of everything he had to Melchizedek, a priest of God Most High. This was a symbol that Abram was making public that he chose God as the Lord of his life, not the king of Sodom who wanted Abram to keep all the goods he had recovered in battle.

Abram would not keep these things that originally belonged to the king of Sodom because Abram didn't want people to get the wrong idea about the source of his prosperity.

The king of Sodom did not provide for Abram; God alone did.

Abram's total dependency on God and the trust that if you give unto God He will provide for all your needs is the philosophy of tithes and offerings.

Tithes and offerings are also a form of pure worship. Why? In this chapter, we will discuss why tithing is an obligation to the Lord, where that command is laid down in scripture and the significance tithing has in someone's faith in God.

We will also discuss why offerings are different from tithes, but still highly important as a form of worship. Both forms of giving illustrate someone's dependence on God and their drive to worship Him through giving.

Tithing is specific

Giving a tenth (or a "tithe") of all you have is referenced early on in the Bible. In the time of Abram (Abraham), when people gave a tithe or a tribute, they were making a statement or a declaration as to what king ruled over their lives.

Tithing unto God is referenced long before the Old Testament Law is established. The Law is not established until Exodus in which God gives Moses basic Judaic Law.

However, way back in Genesis, Abram and Jacob are seen giving tithes and offerings to God. Whenever God would reveal himself to them, Abram (Abraham) and Jacob would always build an altar, present an offering and worship God.

"After Lot had gone, the Lord said to Abram,
'Look as far as you can see in every direction - north

and south, east and west. I am giving all this land, as far as you can see, to you and your descendants as a permanent possession. And I will give you so many descendants that, like the dust of the earth, they cannot be counted! Go and walk through the land in every direction, for I am giving it to you.'

"So Abram moved his camp to Hebron and settled near the oak grove belonging to Mamre. There he built another altar to the Lord." Genesis 13:14-18 (NLT)

"Jacob left Beersheba and traveled toward Haran. At sundown he arrived at a good place to set up camp and stopped there for the night. Jacob found a stone to rest his head against and lay down to sleep. As he slept, he dreamed of a stairway that reached from the earth up to heaven. And he saw the angels of God going up and down the stairway.

"At the top of the stairway stood the Lord, and he said, "I am the Lord, the God of your grandfather Abraham, and the God of your father, Isaac. The ground you are lying on belongs to you. I am giving it to you and your descendants. Your descendants will be as numerous as the dust of the earth! They will spread out in all directions - to the west and the east, to the north and the south. And all the families of the earth will be blessed through you and your descendants. What's more, I am with you,

and I will protect you wherever you go. One day I will bring you back to this land. I will not leave you until I have finished giving you everything I have promised you.

"Then Jacob awoke from his sleep and said, 'Surely the Lord is in this place, and I wasn't aware of it!' But he was also afraid and said, 'What an awesome place this is! It is none other than the house of God, the very gateway to heaven!'

"The next morning Jacob got up very early. He took the stone he had rested his head against, and he set it upright as a memorial pillar. Then he poured olive oil over it. He named that place Bethel (which means 'house of God'), although it was previously called Luz.

"Then Jacob made this vow: 'If God will indeed be with me and protect me on this journey, and if he will provide me with food and clothing, and if I return safely to my father's home, then the Lord will certainly be my God. And this memorial pillar I have set up will become a place of worshiping God, and I will present to God a tenth of everything he gives me.'"
Genesis 28:10-22 (NLT)

These are two good examples - that of Abram (Abraham) and his grandson Jacob - that anchor the concept of tithing theologically. God would remind Abram (Abraham) and

Jacob that He would be with them wherever they went. These men would give tribute to the Lord to signify his protection over them and their devotion to Him. This was their way of saying to God, "Thank you."

Later on in the Old Testament, the Law would be established, which also holds guidelines for tithing to God.

> *"A tithe of everything from the land, whether grain from the soil or fruit from the trees, belongs to the Lord; it is holy to the Lord. If a man redeems any of his tithe, he must add a fifth of the value to it. The entire tithe of the herd and flock - every tenth animal that passes under the shepherd's rod - will be holy to the Lord. He must not pick out the good from the bad or make any substitution. If he does make a substitution, both the animal and its substitution become holy and cannot be redeemed.*
>
> *"These are the commands the Lord gave Moses on Mount Sinai for the Israelites."* Leviticus 27:30-34 (NLT)

A tithe is no less than 10 percent, off of your gross, not net, of what God has blessed you with. This is to be given specifically from your finances. Pastors must teach congregants not to think they can give of their time, but not their tithe. Remember, giving of your time and talent does not supersede the giving of your tithe.

Offering under grace

We no longer live under the Law established in the Old Testament, however, we live under the grace given to us through Jesus' sacrifice on the cross. Christians are not bound by the Judaic law laid down in Exodus. People may use this as an argument not to give ten percent of what they have to God. No one is exempt from the tithe. Remember, Jesus said He did not come to abolish the Law, but to fulfill it.

> *"Do not think that I have come to abolish the Law or the Prophets; I have not come to abolish them but to fulfill them. I tell you the truth, until heaven and earth disappear, not the smallest letter, not the least stroke of a pen, will by any means disappear from the Law until everything is accomplished. Anyone who breaks one of the least of these commandments and teaches others to do the same will be called least in the kingdom of heaven, but whoever practices and teaches these commands will be called great in the kingdom of heaven. For I tell you that unless your righteousness surpasses that of the Pharisees and the teachers of the Law, you will certainly not enter the kingdom of heaven."* Matthew 5:17-20 (NLT)

Jesus lays it out clearly in the New Testament - the Law is as important as ever.

However, it's important that we not forget that Jesus has saved us by His grace. His disciples are giving because they appreciate the gift of grace. A counterargument to those who say we are exempt from giving is this - If you tithe you are only giving 10 percent of all you have. If you give under grace, you should be giving more than 10 percent out of appreciation to Jesus' gift!

Tithing is what we owe back to God when we choose to live under His Kingdom rule. An offering is the overflow of our generosity, given freely and graciously to God.

Giving signifies reliance on God

Tithes and offerings are both forms of giving to God. They are pure acts of worship (not to mention very important acts of worship), but many people might not consider giving when they think about the word "worship." So why is giving considered an act of worship and why is it considered such an important one?

Giving is a form of worship, a tangible act of faith, that demonstrates our total dependence on God for all that we need. Many Christians excel at their prayer life; they excel in reading the Bible and attending services, but what about when it comes to giving?

> *"For I can testify that they gave not only what they could afford, but far more. And they did it of their own free will. They begged us again and again for*

> *the privilege of sharing in the gift for the believers in Jerusalem. They even did more than we had hoped, for their first action was to give themselves to the Lord and to us, just as God wanted them to do. So, we have urged Titus, who encouraged your giving in the first place, to return to you and encourage you to finish this ministry of giving. Since you excel in so many ways—in your faith, your gifted speakers, your knowledge, your enthusiasm, and your love from us—I want you to excel also in this gracious act of giving." 2 Corinthians 8:3-7 (NLT)*

Many disciples struggle when it comes to giving. Why is that?

This is because many people struggle in having faith that God will supply all their needs. This is why tithes and offerings are to be given specifically from your finances, your pocket book. The Bible states:

> *"Where your treasure is, there will your heart be also."* Matthew 6:12 (NLT)

God really does not need our tithes and offerings.

> *"For all the animals of the forest are mine,*
>   *And I own the cattle on a thousand hills."*
> Psalm 50:10 (NLT)

What God cares about is giving what we hold most important (our money) to Him. This act shows that we are not afraid of living without what we give to God, therefore trusting in Him. Giving is a demonstration of faith in God. It is an act of worship that displays complete submission and reliance on God, not on secular materials, to provide for all your needs.

However, this is a concept that many struggle with.

Do not worry about finances

"How will I make ends meet? How will I feed and clothe my family? Where will my next meal come from?"

These are concerns that plague many people. They desire financial security for themselves and their families. If they worry about affording basic necessities, they will almost certainly struggle with giving tithes and offerings. Many people worry that if they give to God as well as buy basic necessities of life, they will have nothing left.

First of all, Jesus assures us not to worry about affording basic necessities.

"Therefore, I tell you, do not worry about your life, what you will eat or drink; or about your body, what you will wear. Is not life more than food, and the body more than clothes? Look at the birds of the air; they do not sow or reap or store away in barns, and yet your heavenly Father feeds them. Are you not much more valuable than they?

Can any one of you by worrying add a single hour to your life?

> *"And why do you worry about clothes? See how the flowers of the field grow. They do not labor or spin. Yet I tell you that not even Solomon in all his splendor was dressed like one of these. If that is how God clothes the grass of the field, which is here today and tomorrow is thrown into the fire, will he not much more clothe you-you of little faith? So do not worry, saying, 'What shall we eat?' or 'What shall we drink?' or 'What shall we wear?' For the pagans run after all these things, and your heavenly Father knows that you need them. But seek first his kingdom and his righteousness, and all these things will be given to you as well. Therefore do not worry about tomorrow, for tomorrow will worry about itself. Each day has enough trouble of its own."* Matthew 6:25-34 (NLT)

Jesus assures us that he will provide for all our basic needs - food, clothing and shelter. Worry over finances should not deter us from giving to the Lord. After all, being poor did not deter the churches in Macedonia from giving. These were impoverished people who gave out of their poverty. In fact, the Apostle Paul had to encourage them to stop giving so generously. Paul put these congregants up as an example to follow for other Christians.

"Now I want you to know, dear brothers and sisters, what God in his kindness has done through the churches in Macedonia. They are being tested by many troubles, and they are very poor. But they are also filled with abundant joy, which has overflowed in rich generosity. For I testify that they gave not only what they could afford, but far more. And they did it of their own free will. They begged us again and again for the privilege of sharing in the gift for the believers in Jerusalem. They even did more than we had hoped, for their first action was to give themselves to the Lord and to us, just as God wanted them to do. So we have urged Titus, who encouraged your giving in the first place, to return to you and encourage you to finish this ministry of giving. Since you excel in so many ways - in your faith, your gifted speakers, your knowledge, your enthusiasm, and your love for us - I want you to excel also in this gracious act of giving." 2 Corinthians 8:1-7 (NLT)

Give out of love, not for reward

However, we should not treat tithes and offerings like a slot machine. Don't expect to give tithes and offerings and become a millionaire. That is not how giving to God works.

You shouldn't give to God expecting to get back in return a bigger house or a new car. We tithe and give offerings because of our love for God. Tithes and offerings are demonstrations of our love and faithfulness to God.

If you open up your eyes every morning and you are in the land of the living, you are already blessed by God. If you give to God, you may still have challenges. The blessings that come from being a faithful and consistent tither should never be confined to more money and/or material things. Just know this: when you tithe and give offerings to God, the blessings you receive back are too numerous to even number. There are more to blessings than just material things.

However, you may receive other blessings from God as well by giving unto Him. If you have a child, should you go out and buy your child nice things to entice or bribe them? No. You should buy things for your child because you love them. However, the more obedient your child is, does that make you even more inclined to bless your child with more things? This is the way God views us when we give to Him.

Giving promotes transparency
Giving is an act of worship for two main reasons: 1. It signifies your utter reliance on God to provide. 2. It also aids in your transparency before God. Worship is all about being completely transparent to God, laying it all on the altar before Him - including one of the things you hold most dear, your money.

Look at Abraham, Isaac, Jacob and Solomon. What you will notice is every time God blessed them they gave back a portion of what God blessed them with. In that they were saying to God, "Everything I have already belongs to you. My house, money, talents and gifts that I have all belong to you." This is called a "faith response." It promotes pure transparency during worship.

In giving to God, you are stating that you don't own yourself. You choose to come under the rule of God and this also includes your bank account. Which belongs to God.

One cannot worship God while holding themselves - or their wealth - back from Him. Giving promotes an open and transparent heart and conscience before the Lord.

God chastises those who selfishly keep their wealth and blessings to themselves without rendering them unto Him.

> *"Will a man rob God? Yet you rob me.*
> *"But you ask, 'How do we rob you?'*
> *"In tithes and offerings. You are under a curse - the whole nation of you - because you are robbing me. Bring the whole tithe into the storehouse, that there may be food in my house. Test me in this,' says the Lord Almighty, 'and see if I will not throw open the floodgates of heaven and pour out so much blessing that you will not have room enough for it. I will prevent pests from devouring your crops, and the vines*

> *in your fields will not cast their fruit,' says the Lord Almighty. 'Then all the nations will call you blessed, for yours will be a delightful land,' says the Lord Almighty."* Malachi 3:8-10 (NLT)

If your house looks beautiful and you are wearing fine clothes, but the house of God looks like a hot mess, God is not going to bless that. He will put holes in your pocket when you try to get ahead. Until you start treating God's house with utmost respect, don't expect your house to be blessed.

I always tell my congregants when we're having an evangelistic outreach effort or fellowship, if they like to drink Coke or Pepsi products, bring them to the outreach or fellowship. Don't bring a knock-off brand - God's house deserves as good as yours, if not better.

Go above and beyond
I encourage my congregation to go above and beyond when it comes to giving. However, everybody in my church does not tithe nor give offerings and I wish they would. They do not for several reasons, the most outstanding being that they don't have faith that God will meet their needs if they give.

But giving should be a joyous time; it shouldn't be viewed as a chore.

I teach my congregants that their worship experience is not complete until they are able to render back to God something. This keeps them mindful why tithes and offerings are an aspect of worship. God promises protection and security to those who are faithful and consistent tithers just as giving makes the worshiper transparent to their Lord.

3

TECHNOLOGY TO SERVE THE PRESENT AGE

"For I am about to do something new. See, I have already begun! Do you not see it? I will make a pathway through the wilderness. I will create rivers in the dry wasteland.

"The wild animals in the fields will thank me, the jackals and owls, too, for giving them water in the desert.

"Yes, I will make rivers in the dry wasteland so my chosen people can be refreshed.

"I have made Israel for myself, and they will someday honor me before the whole world." Isaiah 43:19-21 (NLT)

A favorite old hymn of mine is "A Charge to Keep I Have" by Charles Wesley. Its verse "to serve the present age, my calling to fulfill" rings especially true to me. This verse reminds me that incorporating technology is a great method for growing and maintaining a congregation. Technology also aids in reaching out to the community beyond the church walls.

I believe it goes without saying that technology is increasing by leaps and bounds. It seems as though every other day a new gadget, device or program is being introduced to make our lives easier and more efficient.

However, many churches refuse to use technology to assist with growing their congregation, reaching out to their community, enhancing their worship experience or to increase giving to the church. Many churches still have an upright piano or maybe an organ to incorporate in their worship experience and that's it. They seemingly have no other way to communicate with those beyond their church walls than to leave plain black and white flyers on other people's doors or pass a plate around at offering time for donations of cash and coins.

We must accept this is no longer the church our grandparents grew up in. I am not suggesting that we get rid of what already works. I am suggesting that if you have not been experiencing growth, perhaps you should consider exploring the use of technologies that can assist you. Congregants, pastors, other churches and those in the community will respond positively to utilization of technology within your ministry.

How can my church utilize technology?

Please note there is so much technology out there to the point it can be overwhelming. Remember to avoid getting swept up in trends that seem to change at the blink of an eye. By the time you have become acquainted with one new trend, it seems to become obsolete.

I would suggest exploring and examining technologies that will work for your church's needs and master it. Also remember to tailor technological advances to your church with specific aspects of your congregation and church goals in mind. For example, one elderly member of my congregation pays her tithe with a check every Sunday. That's the way she's always done it and I as her pastor understand that is the way she always will pay her tithe. Another younger congregant, however, doesn't carry cash or checks; she carries a debit or credit card. While there are many millennials who choose to use Cash App.

Remember to offer as many options and be as accommodating as possible when asking others to give to your church.

Utilizing technology in giving

At a recent church conference I attended where the audience was called on to give money, I found only two dollars in my pocket, so what did I do? I whipped out my debit card to give, of course!

Many people just don't carry cash anymore. When the offering plate is passed around during the worship experience, some congregants or anyone who desires to give simply cannot if your church doesn't make some form of giving other than plain old cash available. A church is missing out on so much revenue if they don't accept donations via online technology, smartphone apps or debit/credit cards. There are people out there who want to give so much more than the little cash money in their pockets. However, when the opportunity is offered to them to give to your church they can't. They'll go spend that money elsewhere - such as a football game - that offers a method of currency exchange other than cash.

St. John AME Church offers PayPal for online giving via its website. During worship experiences, debit and credit card giving is encouraged as well as smartphone apps such as Cash App.

PayPal and Cash App make easy efficient exchanges of currency via debit/credit cards. Givelify is another app for church giving and nonprofit donations that can be easily utilized.

These are a few of the many platforms that allow people to give money quickly, efficiently and securely to your church.

There are multiple platform options, not only for giving, but for connecting congregants, raising awareness of an event and outreach to the community. Best of all, like

PayPal, Cash App and Givelify, many of these platforms are completely free for the donor!

How apps can aid your church

Imagine a shopping mall where all of your favorite stores are under one roof. Clothing stores, grocery stores, dry goods, electronics, and books are all available in one enclosed area. You don't have to get in and out of your vehicle, fight traffic or drive place to place to get your shopping done. This shopping mall is a one-stop-shop. This is a good analogy for some very helpful mobile apps that will aid your church. These apps can be downloaded to your smartphone or other mobile devices.

The St. John AME Church mobile app offers everything a congregant or anyone interested in the church will need to explore the aspects of the church. This includes access to the church website, sermons, E-newsletters, forums, church announcements and social media groups.

However, if your budget doesn't allow for an app to be tailored specifically for a certain church there are several platforms available that are all completely free.

Encouraging connectivity through new tech

People now are constantly on the go, some working two or three part-time jobs just to make ends meet. Efficient means of connecting busy congregants and clueing them in immediately on events and happenings is a must for a church. At the other end of the spectrum are those who are shut-in and homebound, unable to go to the church building. However, they still want to participate in the worship experience and church giving.

Technology can provide a solution to reaching out to both the very busy congregants and those who are homebound.

E-newsletters, sent via email weekly, and "all-calls" are very useful in doing this. Text message "blasts," which are sent to multiple phone numbers within your congregation, are a great place to start. These offer news of upcoming events and happenings within the congregation. However, this is only the beginning of what you can do to reach out to your congregation via technology.

St. John AME Livestreams its worship experience through its website. This provides a great interactive means for homebound congregants, as well as those who are out-of-town. Believe me, there are people who desire to worship at your church, yet are unable to reach the church building. This is where utilizing the technology of streaming comes in quite handy to keep people connected.

As one of my homebound congregants says: "Pastor, just because I'm shut-in doesn't mean that I want to be shut-out."

Now, she can log onto her tablet and watch the worship experience live. She can give online almost as easily and efficiently as if she came to the church building.

Mobile apps can aid a church in worship and giving. However, there are other free platforms out there to help a church stream its worship experience live. Facebook Live is one of the most recognizable. Going live online reaches so many people, many of them outside the neighborhood surrounding the actual church building.

Another congregant, who we will call Mr. Withers, had a heart transplant and was in rehabilitation and recovery in a faraway city for three months. However, every Sunday morning, he was watching St. John AME Church's worship experience streaming live on its website. Mr. Withers also participates in Bible study through streaming technology from our church website. New technology has afforded him these opportunities.

Webinars are also a great way of reaching out to others beyond your neighborhood or city. I recently hosted a webinar with other pastors in the AME Church from as far away as Orlando, Florida. Using this platform, I could narrate the presentation and have live conversations with other pastors that would take me hours to reach to meet in person.

The influential role of social media

Social media seems to have taken over our society. Facebook, Twitter, and Snapchat are now household names. "Share," "like," and "tweet" are now part of our daily vocabulary. Many people wouldn't dream of going a day without peeking at their Facebook or Twitter feed on their smartphones.

This helps them keep track of topics important to them or what's going on with family and friends. It goes without saying that social media platforms could and should be incorporated in our church's mission to connect congregants and reach out to our community and world.

Facebook, Twitter, Instagram and Snapchat are all social media platforms that are free to use and reach a wide audience. However, each platform has its benefits and limitations.

Few can deny Facebook and Twitter's wide-reaching scope. These platforms are an incredible way to get the word out on upcoming events and bring awareness to topics at your church. As mentioned before, approach your church's use of technology, including social media, with deference to your congregation and church goal's and specific needs. At St. John AME Church, our use of Facebook tends to reach more people in an older age group. Twitter seems to appeal to a younger audience.

Facebook Live, as mentioned earlier, can stream a worship experience completely free. Your church can have a Facebook page free of charge, but also smaller "group pages" that focus on specific groups within your church. Some churches can host smaller group pages for their women's ministry, choir and youth group.

These smaller group pages can be linked to the main church page on Facebook as well as the church website. These small group pages target congregants in these specific groups. Constantly post things on these small group pages to keep congregants in the loop on upcoming events pertaining to specific groups within the church.

These are also leveraging platforms to bring awareness to a situation out in the community. For example, a church could create a smaller Facebook group page for its Relay for Life team.

Though Facebook seems to loom large within the social media spectrum, other options are available as well including Instagram and Snapchat. These platforms tend towards "spur-of-the-moment" posts and actions. For example, these platforms can only stream live feed for a few moments.

Twitter is another social media giant that reaches countless people. Social media, including Twitter, has inserted the term "hashtag" into our daily vocabulary. This concept, using the "#" sign followed by a word or phrase, can draw major attention to a specific theme, person, circumstance, situation or cause. Churches can employ this to their advantage as well. St. John AME Church has used several hashtags in the past to draw attention to specific church events. The church has an annual theme that focuses on a specific topic and employs a certain hashtag such as: #AllIn #PursueExcellence and #Grow.

I also have my own hashtag: #Worthenworks. I put my hashtag on everything I do or are associated with. It's unique. A quick search for #Worthenworks will bring you directly to my place on the Internet. If you use a hashtag for branding purposes you should make it unique. It's something that's catchy and it helps people find you in the great ocean of the Internet filled with millions of other people, events and ideas.

If creatively named and employed, a hashtag can draw great attention to you and your church goals.

You get what you pay for

Much of the technology mentioned above is free of charge. Many churches run on a tight budget and if funds aren't available, you can begin to up your church's technology game with these free platforms, apps and concepts.

However, there are drawbacks. Listen to St. John AME Church's Livestream worship experience. You cannot hear a baby crying or other background noises. The worship experience will be the only thing you hear during a Livestream broadcast. That is because the streaming service goes directly to a soundboard to filter out background noises and other major distractions. This is a paid service. Churches can pay as little as $99 a month up into the thousands of dollars for this service. There are also no commercials or advertisements competing for viewers' attention when they're watching a worship experience stream live on St. John AME Church's website. Fast Internet connection ensures viewers see a live worship experience stream seamlessly without waiting for a video to load.

A hired website designer creates a site that is navigable, effective and efficient. St. John's website is created by Primecomm Communication out of Florida. I use a graphic designer out of California. These are people I've been doing business with for years, though I don't come into physical contact with them on a daily basis. What you see is the finished product - a streamlined efficient website.

These services could be well worth the investment and yield a great result. Churches that invest aggressively in technology could more than double financially within the span of a few years.

However, a service you pay absolutely nothing for might not yield these results. You get what you pay for. Out-sourcing is OK if you have the budget and you don't have the talent in-house.

Open your mouth and ask!

However, remember to search for the talent that might be hiding in plain sight within your congregation and surrounding community. A motto of mine is: "Open your mouth and ask!"

Perhaps I picked this up from my days as a salesman, but I am not shy about making my needs known and seeking out those who might help me achieve those goals. Work a little harder to incorporate technology into your ministry. I encourage you to get out into your congregation and your community to find people who are tech savvy. St. John

AME offers leadership round-table meetings. During this time, church members are urged to contribute their special skills and talents (which include technology skills) to make our ministry more effective.

Be aggressive! If there is someone I want to get in touch with that I think might have a skill to benefit our ministry, I'll Google their name or search their Facebook page. Sometimes people and things you desire for your ministry might not just come to you. So, I will encourage you to get up, get out and do a little digging to find them.

A person doesn't have to be a genius to start incorporating technology into their ministry. But also keep in mind that all things connected with your church and ministry is your brand. I urge you to be hands-on with all technology used throughout your church because it ultimately reflects on you.

Technology is a tool

Please understand that technology is a tool. It is a useful tool that can enhance someone's worship experience, encourage connectivity within the congregation and community and enable giving in a more efficient manner. However, these gadgets, devices and platforms will never replace one-on-one contact between people. Technology is no substitute for that.

In order to maintain cohesion within your congregation and reach out to the unchurched in the community, you must be personable. You have still got to get out there in your community; you have still got to love people. You have still got to hug people. You have still got to shake hands and smile. You have still got to pray for people. You have still got to love your neighbor as thyself.

Furthermore, don't become a slave shackled to your computer. Set aside time to dedicate to incorporating technology into your church. But, as mentioned previously, don't allow it to overwhelm you or distract you from your church's true mission and goals. There are different tools on specific platforms - such as TweetDeck and Hootsuite - that allow you to schedule automatic posts on social media prior to actually posting it. I could schedule to post a Veterans Day-related tweet in September and it would post automatically in November.

That being said, technology is a very effective tool to enhance a church's outreach of love and compassion. Technology can break down walls and barriers that are created by distance. It has the potential to reach people you might not have thought possible. For example, I know an elderly gentleman in my community - let's call him Walter - who is not a member of St. John AME, but he still calls me "his pastor." And guess who tunes in to see me every Sunday via Livestream? I might have never reached him if not for broadcasting my sermon through this media outlet.

This is a man who literally lives in the same community as the church.

But there are also people tuning in from all over the globe. I recently attended an event in Jamaica. As I was speaking, audience members were on their smartphones contacting me on my various social media platforms! However, it still required my personal touch to allow this to happen.

These examples show you what a powerful tool technology is in reaching out to those near and far. It enables us to serve well in the present age.

4

STRATEGIC COMMUNITY PARTNERSHIPS

"So we have urged Titus, who encouraged your giving in the first place, to return to you and encourage you to finish this ministry of giving. Since you excel in so many ways - in your faith, your gifted speakers, your knowledge, your enthusiasm, and your love from us - I want you to excel also in this gracious act of giving."
2 Corinthians 8:6-7 (NLT)

In the Bible, Paul makes an example of the churches in Macedonia. They were very committed to helping others in need. The people in the churches in Macedonia were quite poor, but that did not inhibit them from giving.

"Now I want you to know, dear brothers and sisters, what God in his kindness has done through

the churches in Macedonia. They are being tested by many troubles, and they are very poor. But they are also filled with abundant joy, which has overflowed in rich generosity.

"For I can testify that they gave not only what they could afford, but far more. And they did it of their own free will. They begged us again and again for the privilege of sharing in the gift for the believers in Jerusalem. They even did more than we had hoped, for their action was to give themselves to the Lord and to us, just as God wanted them to do."
2 Corinthians 8:1-5 (NLT)

Paul frames the congregation in Macedonia as a sterling example of people partnering together and pooling their skills and resources to help those in need. He urges other believers to follow their lead.

"I am not commanding you to do this. But I am testing how genuine your love is by comparing it with the eagerness of the other churches.

"You know the generous grace of our Lord Jesus Christ. Though he was rich, yet for your sake he became poor, so that by his poverty he could make you rich.

"Here is my advice: It would be good for you to finish what you started a year ago. Last year you were the first who wanted to give, and you were the first

to begin doing it. Now you should finish what you started. Let the eagerness you showed in the beginning be matched now by your giving. Give in proportion to what you have. Whatever you give is acceptable if you give it eagerly. And give according to what you have, not what you don't have.

"Of course, I don't mean your giving should make life easy for others and hard for yourselves. I only mean that there should be some equality. Right now you have plenty and can help those who are in need. Later, they will have plenty and can share with you when you need it. In this way, things will be equal. As the Scriptures say, 'Those who gathered a lot had nothing left over, and those who gathered only a little had enough.'" 2 Corinthians 8:8-15 (NLT)

To spread Jesus' gift of eternal life, the "Bread of Life," to others, we must often reach out to them with resources for their day-to-day lives. Food, clothing, fellowship and other necessities can be spread from the church to a hungry and hurting world. Along with these resources, we can also spread the Gospel of Jesus Christ.

But what is the best way to do this?

Strategic partnerships with other organizations in your community is a fantastic way to do this. Alliances with local government, school systems, law enforcement and civic groups offer opportunities ripe to distribute the Bread of Life to those who hunger for food for the body and for the spirit.

What are strategic community partnerships?

Strategic community partnerships are collaborative bodies of individuals and organizations working together on a common goal or issue of importance to the community. It consists of a mutually beneficial relationship where all parties have shared responsibilities, privileges and power. Strategic community partnerships are formed to strengthen the impact of a community education, outreach or advocacy. Therefore, all organizations, churches included, and their objectives benefit from these alliances. In this way, not only does the message of Christ reach the unchurched, but the influence of the church is expanded into other entities within the community.

Environment/personality influence partnerships

While reading forward in this chapter, please keep three points in mind.

The partnerships churches forge with other organizations depend largely on the environment in which they exist. Eufaula, Alabama, the city in which I pastor, is a smaller more rural community than, say, Atlanta. It is by no means a metropolitan area. This has its advantages as well as its drawbacks.

In a metropolitan area like Atlanta, you may not have immediate access to the mayor's office or police chief as you would in a smaller city like Eufaula. However, Eufaula does not have a homeless shelter, YMCA or soup kitchen, so, of course, prospective partnerships with these entities are not possible. In a more rural setting, your church may be forced to get more creative in forming alliances.

Second, remember as you move forward forming alliances between your church and other community entities, that the personality of your church will play a big role in this area of growth. For example, St. John AME Church does not send missionaries on trips abroad to developing countries. The church is simply not equipped for these outreach programs as a much larger church might be. We know that, so we focus on other areas of outreach closer to home, so to speak. When you intimately understand the personality and resources of your church, you will begin to realize the partnerships your church is capable of.

Third, do not become overwhelmed trying to reach out to every need you see in your community or in creating alliances with every community organization. Find your niche partnerships. Focus on them and make them thrive. Do not try to be everything to everyone because you will get bogged down in responsibilities and burned out.

Food/clothing programs
Feeding programs are an excellent form of outreach to the unchurched. They can also forge partnerships with

community organizations. As mentioned above, Eufaula has no homeless shelter or soup kitchen, but that doesn't mean there aren't people in the community hungry for food to nourish their body and spirit. Take the kids who benefit from our feeding program, for example.

St. John AME Church has a summer feeding program that offers hot meals to more than 400 children in the Eufaula area for five days a week during their summer vacation. The children who come to the St. John AME Church campus aren't the only kids being fed. Meals are shuttled out to daycare centers and to the Eufaula Boys & Girls Club.

This program is part of a strategic community partnership with the State of Alabama as well as the City of Eufaula. The city government provides shuttle buses to deliver meals to children who cannot come to the church campus for lunch. This partnership provides summer jobs to people as well. The people who drive the shuttle buses and the people who cook the food at St. John AME are all paid individuals, so this strategic community partnership is contributing to the local economy.

This partnership also extends to other churches. Some churches just don't have the infrastructure to hold a summer feeding program for their young people. A solution to their problem is partnering with another church - St. John AME Church. During the summer feeding program, St. John AME has partnered with three other churches. These churches notify their youth of the St. John AME feeding program and St. John picks them up at these churches to carry them to our campus to feed them.

In return, these churches aid St. John AME in various ways with the summer feeding program. One year our van stopped working and New Mount Zion AME Church volunteered their van to help in picking up kids and distributing meals.

Another city partnership St. John AME fosters is with Eufaula City Schools. St. John AME has a feeding ministry for the school system's basketball program. Before many home games, the church feeds the varsity basketball team, junior varsity basketball team, girls varsity basketball, varsity cheerleaders and coaching staff. The food is donated by St. John AME congregants.

"Helping Hands" is another St. John AME program to provide clothing through a partnership with Walmart. These clothes are surplus to the store and provided free of charge to anyone in need. The program provides clothing for infants all the way up to adults. These are brand new clothes that still have the tags on them.

This is an alliance built on trust and a drive to help our community. We have a partnership with Walmart; Walmart trusts St. John AME to do right by folks in need.

This program requires no ID from prospective recipients. St. John AME Church doesn't ask them to pay for anything. Imagine how many people this is be a blessing to, especially if these people are single mother's on minimum wage with two kids or someone who has lost all they own in a natural catastrophe or other disaster.

Educational programs

When a church teaches practical skills and educational programs, this is also a good opportunity for strategic community partnerships.

St. John AME hosts "Keys to Financial Success" which is the first in a series of educational programs the church sponsors. This program teaches financial literacy and is open to the community. All people, not just congregants, are welcome to take part in this program. More on this program will be covered in the chapter on holistic ministry. However, this educational program forges partnerships with many different financial institutions in the community to make this educational program a reality.

Different credit organizations, realtors, banks, discount brokers and investors partner with St. John AME Church to teach information on different financial subjects. These representatives of different financial institutions are guest speakers during the "Keys to Financial Success" program. They teach on different financial aspects in an effort to make people in the community financially literate. St. John AME Church's objective is to teach people about managing their finances from a Biblical perspective. Through this strategic community partnership, both the church and these financial institutions benefit by teaching people

God's Word on finances and creating more financially literate people.

Health care outreach

Those in hospitals and other health care facilities are often hurting physically. They may also be in spiritual pain. This is an excellent opportunity for a church to form a partnership with health care organizations as a means of outreach to those suffering.

St. John AME Church partners with Medical Center Barbour, Eufaula's local hospital, to provide snacks and other refreshments to caregivers and family members of patients.

Every Monday, we go into the local nursing home and have a worship experience for the patients and staff. This has been done by St. John AME Church for at least a decade. This involves singing, scripture-reading, Bible teaching and prayer.

During National Nurses Week in the month of May St. John AME sponsors a cookout at the hospital and the nursing home to feed all the faculty and staff there.

Chamber/community partnerships

St. John AME has formed alliances with the Eufaula Chamber of Commerce and a variety of civic organizations. During the past few years, St. John AME has had the largest number of volunteers during the Martin Luther

King Day of Community Service, sponsored by the Eufaula Chamber of Commerce.

Our "Silver Edition" ministry provides opportunities for senior citizens throughout the community to gather for fellowship. This ministry is open to all senior citizens in the community, not just congregants of our church. This is another ministry that reaches out to the community.

The church is always making itself visible within the community. We participate in and partner with the annual Barbour County Relay for Life; we take part in the Relay for Life Cancer Walk each year. This event draws awareness to cancer patients, cancer treatment, cancer survivors, cancer research and cancer research fund-raising.

We also have congregants as representatives at Indian Summer and the Eufaula Pilgrimage, two big annual events in our community. We have people out there every year offering Polish dogs, chips and sodas. This makes the church visible and accessible to people beyond the church walls. It's all about reaching out to others in a straightforward and uncomplicated way.

How to create and fund partnerships

As a pastor, I trust my congregants to come to me with their ideas of potential community partnerships. Few people will know the needs of their neighbors better than your congregation. Our alliance with the Eufaula City Schools basketball program, for example, came about through a congregant's idea. Their son played on the varsity basketball team.

A good leader and pastor listens carefully to those around them. They recognize their congregants' skills to identify needs and their ideas for addressing them. Therefore, keep not only your eyes, but your ears open too.

CDC and CDO

In creating strategic community partnerships, the church can possibly birth a CDC (Community Development Corporation) or a CDO (Community Development Organization). This, however, is something that should not be entered into lightly. Skilled individuals should participate in assisting you with setting this up the proper way.

The same can be said about acquiring grants, donations and in-kind resources for your church outreach programs and partnerships. A competent skilled staff is needed to acquire these funds.

Avoid "Lone Ranger" Syndrome

Backpack drives, voter registration and Easter egg hunts are community outreach programs many churches, it seems, want to do. This creates such an unnecessary overlap by churches within the faith community.

Churches and civic organizations at times compete to make these programs available. They go at it alone in a sort of "Lone Ranger" Syndrome. This is when a person or organization chooses to enter into tasks without building coalitions from other missionally aligned people and/or organizations. This often has limited to no impact. Services become fragmented as different organizations each strive to hold the same event instead of pooling their time and resources.

In fact, those in need may find it more difficult to reach these services due to this scattered nature. However, this can also be an opportunity for the wise. When churches and civic clubs come together - especially in smaller communities with less resources - on a specific outreach program, they can reach many more people.

Two years ago, St. John AME Church partnered with two other local churches, Zion Baptist Church and New Covenant Ministries, as well as the Buffalo Soldiers motorcycle club to host a community-wide Easter egg hunt. With this partnership, we reached an overwhelming number of children and their parents - far more than we could have going it alone.

Be visible, be straightforward
During both our summer feeding program and the feeding program for the Eufaula City Schools basketball program, we open with a prayer and close with a prayer. As these kids park their feet under the table, we extend an invitation to them and their families to join our congregation. When we reach out to healthcare providers, hospital patients and

nursing home residents and staff, we provide the same straightforward message. When we chat with festival-goers or give clothes to a needy family, our message is the same - we offer spiritual comfort and a prospective church home.

The examples above are by no means an exhaustive list of strategic community partnerships for community outreach. There is a plethora of opportunities for alliances available in your community. However, approach them in a similar manner.

Be straightforward. Pick up the telephone and make contacts. Knock on doors. Visit the offices of city leaders. Call or stop by civic groups and clubs. Let community leaders know that your church is eager to forge partnerships in addressing needs in the community. Ask how your church can help.

Strategic community partnerships give the church moral authority and influence in the community. Partnerships are one way to carry out a ministry of giving that Jesus Christ charged us with.

> *"But when the Son of Man comes in his glory, and all the angels with him, then he will sit upon his glorious throne. All the nations will be gathered in his presence, and he will separate the people as a shepherd separates the sheep and the goats. He will place the sheep at his right hand and the goats at his left.*

> *"Then the King will say to those on his right,*
> *'Come, you who are blessed by my Father, inherit*
> *the Kingdom prepared for you from the creation of*
> *the world. For I was hungry, and you fed me. I was*
> *thirsty, and you gave me a drink. I was a stranger,*
> *and you invited me into your home. I was naked, and*
> *you gave me clothing. I was sick, and you cared for me.*
> *I was in prison, and you visited me.'*
>
> *"Then these righteous ones will reply, 'Lord, when*
> *did we ever see you hungry and feed you? Or thirsty*
> *and give you something to drink? Or a stranger and*
> *show you hospitality? Or naked and give you cloth-*
> *ing? When did we ever see you sick or in prison and*
> *visit you?'*
>
> *"And the King will say, 'I tell you the truth, when*
> *you did it to one of the least of these my brothers and*
> *sisters, you were doing it to me!'"* Matthew 25:31-40
> (NLT)

However, the church cannot help the community or establish influence in the community if the church is not involved in the community.

Get out there! Present a vision to community leaders they can buy into, but don't make it complicated. Be your authentic self to gain the trust of both community leaders and those in need. Once you gain a reputation as being trustworthy and getting things done, others may come to you as well.

Strategic community partnerships are all about moving your church beyond its four walls.

5

HOLISTIC MINISTRY

"For I was hungry and you gave me food, I was thirsty and you gave me drink, I was a stranger and you welcomed me, I was naked and you clothed me, I was sick and you visited me, I was in prison and you came to me.' Then the righteous will answer him saying, 'Lord, when did we see you hungry and feed you, or when did we see you thirsty and give you drink? And when did we see you a stranger and welcome you, or naked and clothe you? And when did we see you sick or in prison and visit you?' And the King will answer them, 'Truly, I say to you, as you did it to one of the least of my brothers you did it to me.'" Matthew 25:35-40 (NLT)

Christ commissioned his children to go out and spread his teachings to all the world and share with everyone His gift of salvation. This is known as the Great Commission.

> *"Jesus came and told his disciples, 'I have been given authority in heaven and on Earth. Therefore, go and make disciples of all the nations, baptizing them in the name of the Father and the Son and the Holy Spirit. Teach these new disciples to obey all the commands I have given you. And be sure of this: I am with you always, even to the end of the age."*
> Matthew 28:16-20 (NLT)

We are expected to offer all others the Bread of Life through Christ Jesus. However, we are also expected to nurture people in their minds, bodies and relationships as well. Christians must give people in need practical skills and resources for navigating this life.

People are hurting and dying right before our very eyes. Sometimes these people are in physical pain. Others suffer from mental or psychological trauma. The majority of these people are spiritually lost; they need the gift of Jesus Christ's salvation for their souls. However, as children of God, we have the opportunity to show compassion to these hurting people. We can do this, of course, by sharing with them Jesus' gift of salvation. But we also have the power to alleviate their pain in this world - physical, mental, psychological and spiritual - to at least some degree.

This philosophy is the heart and soul of holistic ministry. Holistic ministry offers compassion, empathy, care and above all Christ to those within and outside the four walls of the church. Holistic ministry also teaches practical advice and skills to others to help them throughout this life.

The holistic ministry approach gives a hungry person a loaf of bread, the ability to get more bread and, above all, the Bread of Life.

Compassionate care

In the Bible, the Lord condemns those who turn a blind eye or a deaf ear to those in need:

> "Then the King will turn to those on the left and say, 'Away with you, you cursed ones, into the eternal fire prepared for the devil and the demons. For I was hungry, and you didn't feed me. I was thirsty, and you didn't give me a drink. I was a stranger, and you didn't invite me into your home. I was naked, and you didn't give me clothing. I was sick and in prison, and you didn't visit me.'
>
> "Then they will reply, 'Lord, when did we ever see you hungry or thirsty or a stranger or in prison, and not help you?'
>
> "And he will answer, 'I will tell you the truth, when you refused to help the least of these my brothers and sisters, you were refusing to help me.'

> *"And they will go away into eternal punish-*
> *ment, but the righteous will go into eternal life."*
> Matthew 25: 41-46 (NLT)

Compassion is at the core of holistic ministry. Compassion is defined as the sympathy and concern for the suffering or misfortunes of others. The Bible tells us that the world is always ripe with opportunities to aid the sick, lonely and unfortunate and that, as God's children, we are called on to help them.

> *"But if there are any poor in your towns when you*
> *arrive in the land the Lord your God is giving you,*
> *do not be hard-hearted or tightfisted toward them.*
> *Instead, be generous and lend them whatever they*
> *need. Do not be mean-spirited and refuse some-*
> *one a loan because the year for canceling debts is*
> *close at hand. If you refuse to make the loan and*
> *the needy person cries out to the Lord, you will*
> *be considered guilty of sin. Give generously to the*
> *poor, not grudgingly, for the Lord your God will*
> *bless you in everything you do. There will always*
> *be some in the land who are poor. That is why I*
> *am commanding you to share freely with the poor*
> *and with others in need."* Deuteronomy 15:7-11
> (NLT)

This means helping the unfortunate by feeding and clothing them, but also by offering a listening, empathetic ear and fellowship to the lonely, the sick and the elderly.

Providing for the physical body

In the previous chapter on strategic community partnerships, I discussed how St. John AME Church partners with local government, school systems, civic organizations and other churches in Eufaula, the town where I currently pastor. In these partnerships, the church has a greater opportunity of reaching as many people as possible to share the gift of Christ's salvation. The best way to spread the Gospel, however, is often through offering the necessities of this life: food, clothing, and shelter.

Feeding the hungry could be one of the simplest acts of compassion. People require bread as well as the Bread of Life. Some people may very well have never been inside of a church. Giving them food when they are hungry and in need is an excellent time to also introduce Jesus' gift of salvation. If the hungry cannot provide food for themselves, chances are they have other troubles too - including spiritual turmoil.

There are few better ways to break down barriers between a disciple of Christ and a spiritually lost individual than over a good, hot meal. This is also a fantastic way to aid someone in the body and the spirit.

St. John AME Church is located in an area where there are many low-income families with young children. During the school year, many of these children qualify for a free-lunch program at their schools. During the summer, however, a hot lunch might not be available to them.

This is where St. John AME Church's summer feeding program comes into play. For more than a decade, St. John AME has been providing 400-500 meals to children for five days a week during summer vacation. This provides a good, hot meal to children who are brought to the church or who walk to the church from the community surrounding St. John AME. That, however, isn't where this ministry stops.

Hot meals are also delivered to local daycare centers and the Eufaula Boys & Girls Club. We are also in partnership with five other local churches to get hot meals to their youth. These churches are considerably smaller and do not have the infrastructure to support a summer feeding program. It is just more cost efficient for them to let St. John AME bring food to their church location. In partnering with St. John AME Church, their kids are fed as well.

The St. John AME Church summer feeding program is also a holistic ministry in providing jobs to people throughout the summer vacation. The transit buses that shuttle the meals to daycare centers, Boys & Girls Club and other church campuses are driven by paid employees of the City of Eufaula. The people who prepare the food at St. John AME Church are paid individuals too.

The summer feeding program not only helps those in need of food, but those in need of jobs.

Food and clothing are the basic necessities of life. Imagine losing everything you own in a natural disaster or other catastrophe like a fire. Or imagine being a single mom with children constantly in need of clothing and shoes to fit their rapidly growing bodies.

This is where St. John AME Church's "Helping Hands" program comes into play. Some charities require proof of income to distribute clothing to the needy. Therefore, those in the most desperate need have to wait for a substantial amount of time before receiving clothing they need right away. This is not so with Helping Hands.

This ministry is part of a partnership with Walmart. Walmart provides new clothing for infants to adults of all sizes. St. John AME Church distributes them to anyone who contacts the church in need. St. John AME asks them to pay nothing at all.

Teaching practical skills

Have you ever heard the saying? "Give a person a fish, the person eats for one day. Teach the person to fish, the person eats for a lifetime." Oftentimes, a church will help someone pay a bill, but not teach them to manage what God has blessed them with. God expects us to be good stewards of our resources and relationships. Holistic ministry also includes offering practical knowledge to people in need of life skills and advice.

St. John AME Church has recently started a ministry called "Keys to Financial Success." This is part of an ongoing ministry series at our church that teaches "keys" to managing lifestyles - such as the keys to healthy eating, financial success and loving marriage.

Keys to Financial Success is the first in this series. Its goal is to educate people throughout the community on financial literacy.

So many people in our communities have little to no savings. They only have enough income to survive from paycheck to paycheck. It's sad. Think of a 60-year-old person who has worked hard since they were 20 years old. They don't even have 5,000 dollars in their bank account. It's not that they haven't earned that money over the past decades, but they have inadequate knowledge of saving, investing, budgeting or wisely spending their money.

Wealth is built little by little. If we are the good stewards God expects us to be we will notice a difference in our bank accounts. Keys to Financial Success is all about teaching people about managing their finances from a Biblical perspective while still providing them with practical advice.

This ministry is a partnership with several different financial institutions in our community including realtors, bankers, investors, financial planners, mortgage brokers, insurance agents and credit organizations. These people are guest speakers during this ministry, teaching people about credit utilization scores, credit cards versus debit cards, understanding credit scores, saving and investing, mortgages and homeownership among other financial topics. This ministry also stresses the importance of health insurance, life insurance and renter's insurance.

Soothing the soul

Hunger can come in many forms. Sometimes it comes from the stomach wanting food. Sometimes it involves the mind hungering for knowledge. At other times, people hunger for companionship and love. There are many lonely people in the world. If you are wondering how far you have to look to find sad and lonely people to minister to, chances are there might be one sitting right next to you. Holistic ministry is as much about lifting people's spirits as it is about feeding the body.

Give someone a smile, a kind word, a visit or just a note or letter telling them you care. These compassionate gestures often mean as much (if not more) than a hot meal or suitable clothing to someone in need.

Actively integrating ministries to minister to and cheer the hearts of the lonely, sick, shut-in, homesick and homebound is an integral part of a church's holistic ministry.

Fellowship is necessary

No matter their age, people can feel emotions of isolation and loneliness. It is as important to let a young child know they are valued and loved as it is a homebound elderly person.

St. John AME Church has holistic ministries for people of every age. Each of these ministries is designed to minister to different age groups throughout our community. They all have one thing in common, however. They all minister to lonely and hurting people through fellowship.

We have sponsored youth outings in which congregants purchase tickets and snacks for young children to go to the movies. These children may not be able to afford this treat otherwise.

Our Silver Edition ministry touches senior citizens who gather once a month to fellowship with each other. The ministry is open to all senior citizens in the community.

Our "Sons of Allen" men's ministry is an opportunity for men to gather at Lakepoint, a state park and resort in Eufaula, once a month to have fellowship, just guys being guys.

"Faithful Few" is open to seniors and older adults. This ministry meets once a month to take seniors on outings and other trips.

All of these ministries are open to everyone in the community; you don't have to be a St. John AME congregant to participate. These holistic ministries are about getting people up, out of the house and in an environment where they feel loved and valued.

Feeding, clothing and educating people is important, but fellowship is just as necessary to keep someone happy and healthy.

Outreach to those shut-in, far away

People in need of compassion and support often cannot physically come to the church, so the church must come to them.

Our "Congregational Care" ministry mails out care packages to people in the military, college and others far away from home. This ministry doesn't just send them necessities and treats, but also a message that we are praying for them. Though they are far away, they receive a clear message that they are valued and cared for.

Congregational Care also makes a point to visit the sick and shut-in in our community regularly. Those participating in this ministry not only pray for and with these homebound individuals, they help them get to doctors' appointments, make sure they're getting their proper medications and do chores and other projects for them as needed.

Perhaps our most longtime holistic ministry is our nursing home ministry. St. John AME has had this ministry for more than a decade. On Monday mornings, we hold a worship experience at the local nursing home for both the residents and the staff. This involves singing, scripture-reading, Bible teaching and prayer.

People in nursing homes can be some of the loneliest people in society. They may receive only sporadic visits from their children, other family members and friends. Their physical health may be in decline and these feelings of loneliness and isolation do not do their emotional state any favors. Singing and fellowship gives them something to look forward to and participate in. These ministries also let them know that they are not forgotten about; they are still a valued and cherished part of society.

Holistic ministry ministers to the whole person, not just the spiritual person. Ministries that help and encourage the sick, elderly, homebound and homesick send a clear message that these people do not have to lead their lives in stifling isolation.

Identify needs, stay focused

As with strategic community partnerships, the list is virtually endless as to what your church can do as far as holistic ministries go.

When considering the vast needs of people around you, this can seem overwhelming. How do you begin to identify which needs beyond your church walls warrant a holistic ministry from your church? Well, first off, listen to and observe what the people around you are going through.

For example, if there is a high illiteracy rate in your area, you might want to consider designing a literacy advocacy ministry. If the area you live in has a particular recreational activity or tourism draw its known for consider building a fellowship ministry through that. Eufaula is known for its sprawling lake and its big bass fishing; a fishing ministry that encourages fellowship and outreach through this sport could be a good idea.

Know your area intimately. Understand your environment and current events. Take for example the people in the Florida panhandle recovering from Hurricane Michael. They have all kinds of construction workers rebuilding from the damage done by this natural disaster. Here is a fine opportunity for a construction ministry; a congregation could carry sandwiches and beverages to the people rebuilding from the storm.

Second, take the pulse of your congregation and your community. Listen carefully to your congregants. Few people know your community and its needs better than your church. Our Silver Edition ministry, for example, was born out of our senior congregants partnering with others in the community to create a support system for local senior citizens.

The personality of your church will define what sorts of holistic ministries you are capable of. As I mentioned in the previous chapter, our church does not send missionaries to countries abroad because we know we cannot support that ministry. A larger church who has the capacity could be better suited to facilitate this ministry, but we cannot. However, a smaller church could comfortably facilitate a summer feeding program for local youth with great success.

That is why it is so important to listen earnestly to your congregation and community. They will guide you to what needs in the community require addressing and what your church is capable of.

More importantly, don't become overwhelmed by biting off more than you can chew. Identify and focus on one specific need or a few specific needs according to what your church infrastructure can support. There is a fine balance between overdoing it and not being effective and doing a few specific ministries and being very effective.

Third, make holistic ministries interactive, personable and, above all else, fun! I have a personal motto concerning holistic ministry. This is "food, fellowship, prayer and fun." You have got to have those four things in order to have a good ministry. Fellowship and fun will break the ice and break down barriers for people you are trying to reach to help and share Jesus' plan of salvation. Besides who doesn't like a good meal?

More than prayer

Holistic ministry involves practices that sustain people the church seeks to reach out to. A suffering person may get a euphoric worship experience on Sunday morning. However, their life still feels broken and in shambles after church is over. This is because they are not equipped with practical information nor do they have a loving support system to fellowship with and help them.

Holistic ministry is a ministry that states to someone suffering, "We will not just pray for you - we will help you practically as well."

Holistic ministry is also about moving the church beyond its four walls. Every one of the above examples are literally carrying the church beyond our street address to meet the physical and social needs throughout the community. These are ministries that impact daily lives on a practical level.

ABOUT THE AUTHOR

Carlton Worthen is a "Florida Boy," and is the oldest child of Rev. & Mrs. Charlie C. Worthen. Carlton was born and raised in the Capital City of Tallahassee, Florida, and attended the prestigious Florida A&M University (FAMU). Carlton received his Bachelor of Science Degree in Political Science, with a minor in Public Administration. Carlton has his Master of Divinity Degree (M.Div.) from Turner Theological Seminary of The Interdenominational Theological Center (ITC), with a concentration in Homiletics and Worship, and was commended for receiving one of the highest honors in his class.

Carlton was known as one of Tallahassee's favorite talk show hosts, as the host of *"C.W. Presents."* He brought fresh perspectives that were both engaging and entertaining to his audience. In 2004, Carlton produced and hosted a city-wide symposium in Tallahassee, Florida, *"Make Your Vote*

Count." The symposium was targeted to individuals encouraging them to turn out and vote during the 2004 presidential elections between President George W. Bush and Senator John Kerry.

Carlton's many accomplishments have included being a top adviser to former Mayor/Commissioner of Tallahassee, Dorothy Inman-Johnson, providing volunteer and consulting services to U.S. Representative Allan Boyd, D-Florida, Leon County Commissioner Cliff Thaell and to former candidate for the Leon County Commission, Bob Henderson. Worthen has also served on the Board of Directors for the 2-1-1 Big Bend, a subsidiary of The United Way.

Carlton has always had a love for God and a passion for God's word. Carlton accepted his calling in 2005, and thus strives to fulfill God's calling on his life. In 2007, Carlton was selected to participate in ITC's distinguished program "Faith Journey", a program which selects only the "chosen few" students who demonstrate superb academic excellence and extraordinary promise in parish ministry.

In 2008, God encouraged Carlton to begin "The Empowerment Ministries" in Atlanta, Georgia, and charged Carlton to plant this ministry into the lives of others. "The Empowerment Ministries" is a ministry that seeks to foster uninhibited and dynamic praise and worship, social and political activism, and dedicated service to the community, empowerment to pastors and congregations, and financial growth.

In 2011, Carlton was elected by the Turner Theological Seminary Alumni/ae to serve as their national President.

In 2012, Carlton provided the keynote address to the Barnesville, Georgia Lamar county NAACP Annual Banquet.

Currently, Carlton is the Senior Pastor of St. John A.M.E. Church in Eufaula, Alabama.

Carlton lives by the motto, *"Be prosperous in all that you do."* Carlton spends his spare time watching comedy movies, reading, resting on the sandy beaches of Florida and attending FAMU football games.

Made in the USA
Columbia, SC
15 August 2023

21699604R00055